SEASONS OF FUN: SUMMER

by Finley Fraser

Consultant: Beth Gambro
Reading Specialist, Yorkville, Illinois

Minneapolis, Minnesota

Teaching Tips

Before Reading

- Look at the cover of the book. Discuss the picture and the title.

- Ask readers to brainstorm a list of what they already know about summer holidays. What can they expect to see in the book?

- Go on a picture walk, looking through the pictures to discuss vocabulary and make predictions about the text.

During Reading

- Read for purpose. Encourage readers to think about the special days in summer as they are reading.

- Ask readers to look for the details of the book. What is happening on these days?

- If readers encounter an unknown word, ask them to look at the sounds in the word. Then, ask them to look at the rest of the page. Are there any clues to help them understand?

After Reading

- Encourage readers to pick a buddy and reread the book together.

- Ask readers to name three summer holidays from the book. Go back and find the pages that tell about these things.

- Ask readers to write or draw something they learned about summer holidays.

Credits:

Cover and title page, © Sara Winter/Shutterstock; 3, © Pixel- Shot/Shutterstock; 5, © Rawpixel.com/Shutterstock; 6–7, © Robert Kneschke/Shutterstock; 9, © Anthony Correia/Shutterstock; 11, © fstop123/iStock; 12–13, © Bastiaan Slabbers/iStock; 15, © Megan Betteridge/Shutterstock; 16, © Nikada/iStock; 17, © kali9/iStock; 18–19, © Antonio_Diaz/iStock; 21, © M_a_y_a/iStock; 22T, © Everett Collection/Shutterstock; 22M, © timfazyl/Shutterstock; 22B, © Richard Levine/Alamy; 23TL, © duncan1890/iStock; 23TM, © Dana.S/Shutterstock; 23TR, © Roberto Galan/iStock; 23BL, © Png- Studio/iStock; 23BM, © michaeljung/Shutterstock; and 23BR, © bauhaus1000/iStock.

Library of Congress Cataloging-in-Publication Data

Names: Fraser, Finley, 1972- author.
Title: Summer holidays / by Finley Fraser ; Consultant: Beth Gambro,
Reading Specialist, Yorkville, Illinois.
Description: Bearport Publishing. | Minneapolis, Minnesota : Bearport
Publishing Company, [2023] | Series: Seasons of fun: summer | Includes
bibliographical references and index.
Identifiers: LCCN 2022025648 (print) | LCCN 2022025649 (ebook) | ISBN
9798885093293 (library binding) | ISBN 9798885094511 (paperback) | ISBN
9798885095662 (ebook)
Subjects: LCSH: Holidays--Juvenile literature. | Summer--Juvenile
literature. | Juneteenth--Juvenile literature.
Classification: LCC GT3933 .F73 2023 (print) | LCC GT3933 (ebook) | DDC
394.26--dc23
LC record available at https://lccn.loc.gov/2022025648
LC ebook record available at https://lccn.loc.gov/2022025649

Copyright © 2023 Bearport Publishing Company. All rights reserved. No part of this publication may be reproduced in whole or in part, stored in any retrieval system, or transmitted in any form or by any means, electronic, mechanical, photocopying, recording, or otherwise, without written permission from the publisher.

For more information, write to Bearport Publishing, 5357 Penn Avenue South, Minneapolis, MN 55419.

Contents

Holiday Fun 4

The Story of Juneteenth 22

Glossary 23

Index 24

Read More 24

Learn More Online 24

About the Author 24

Holiday Fun

It is time for summer fun!

There are many fun days in the summer.

Some of them are holidays.

I love summer holidays.

For many, Memorial Day marks the start of summer.

It comes at the end of May.

We honor people in the United States **military**.

I watch my grandpa march in a **parade** on Memorial Day.

He was in the military a long time ago.

I am very **proud** of him.

Father's Day is in June.

It is a day all about dads!

I give my dad a card and a gift.

We spend the day together.

We remember freedom from **slavery** in June.

June 19 is called Juneteenth.

People come together and eat.

They play music and dance, too!

My brother loves the Fourth of July!

This is the day the United States became a country.

There is a parade in my town.

I get together with my family on this day.

We eat a big dinner.

Then, we watch **fireworks** light up the sky!

Labor Day is the first Monday in September.

We think about all that working people do for us.

Now, summer is over.

Summer holidays are fun.

I love them all!

Which summer holiday do you like best?

The Story of Juneteenth

In 1863, President Abraham Lincoln said all **enslaved** people were free.

This news did not get to everyone right away. The people of Galveston, Texas, finally heard about it on June 19, 1865.

Now, we remember this day every year. It is also called Freedom Day.

Glossary

enslaved made to work without being paid

fireworks things that explode in the sky and make lights and sounds

military having to do with armies or war

parade people walking together for a celebration

proud very happy because of something that has been done

slavery forcing people to work for no pay

Index

fireworks 16
freedom 12, 22
military 6, 8
music 12
parades 8, 14
United States 6, 14

Read More

Koestler-Grack, Rachel. *Juneteenth (Blastoff! Readers: Celebrating Holidays).* Minneapolis: Bellwether Media, Inc., 2019.

Potter, Jonathan. *Why Do We Celebrate Independence Day? (Celebrating U.S. Holidays).* New York: PowerKids Press, 2019.

Learn More Online

1. Go to **www.factsurfer.com** or scan the QR code below.
2. Enter "**Summer Holidays**" into the search box.
3. Click on the cover of this book to see a list of websites.

About the Author

Finley Fraser is a writer living in Portland, Maine. He's known for his very good Fourth of July barbecues and his very bad jokes.